Heather Manley, N.D.
www.drheathernd.com

As parents, our sincerest hope for our children is that they will learn to make good choi[ces] nourishing their bodies and minds with all the good things this world has to offer them. [...] as a mother of two and creator of **weelicious.com**, I am all too aware that trying to get k[ids] excited about food and what goes in their bodies is not an easy feat.

From the first time I encountered Human Body Detectives, I knew I had discovered something special and found a kindred spirit in Dr. Heather. Dr. Heather's Human Body Detectives series [are] great stories written with a heart and sense of humor that engages and educates kids by inspir[ing] them to be healthy, eat well and, most of all, have fun doing it. In fact, "Fun" is the operative word. The good habits and healthy practices your kids will learn in **Human Body Detectives** are just the by products of the good time they will have reading it. This series, about the importance of kids respecting their own bodies, is one of the greatest gifts you can give your children and one that they will in turn be able to give themselves everyday they employ the lessons learned in the pages of Dr. Heather's books.

I wish learning was this fun when I was a kid!

Catherine McCord
Founder, weelicous.com

human body detectives®

Battle with the Bugs

CASE FILE #2

Dr. Heather Manley

"The man beside us was sneezing and coughing the whole flight. I hope neither of the boys get sick," Merrin overheard her Aunt Lindsay say.

It was spring break and Merrin and Pearl had just met up with their cousins, aunts and uncles in Mexico. The flight was long, but now that they were all together, it was worth the trip.

All were happy in their big rented beach house until their littlest cousin, Max, started to cry. It was a sad cry. A cry for help. He was turning red, pulling his ears. He was in pain.

Merrin and Pearl looked at each other and knew they had to help him. Pearl turned to her cousin Sam and began whispering. Merrin grew worried.

Was Pearl telling him their secret?

1

They needed to find out what was wrong with Max.

THERE WAS NO TIME TO WASTE!

Quickly, Merrin ran over to Pearl

and pulled her aside.

"*COME ON!* We need to go. We can tell everyone that we're tired from the trip and going to take a nap," Merrin explained.

"We need to bring Sam. Sam said that he was just really sick, too, right before the trip. Maybe he can help us find out what's wrong with Max," said Pearl.

Merrin imagined doing their human body detective work with another kid and smiled. "Maybe it is a good idea. Go get him and meet me in our room."

Before any explanation could be made to Sam, Merrin and Pearl closed their eyes and visualized themselves in baby Max's body. They were not sure where in his body, but their desire to help him was strong. They felt a pull as the dizziness settled in. Sam looked white but he was used to being in strange predicaments, like when he was left at home alone by mistake. As soon as he saw the smiles on his cousins' faces, he relaxed, until... the soft, mushy landing.

They all opened their eyes slowly. It was dark but not quite black. It was like they were in a tunnel; they could see some light. They tried to move their feet but the goopy green stuff they were standing in made it really difficult. Along with the sticky goop were some hair-like things that were trying hard to sway back and forth.

"What the heck!" Sam yelled. "Where are we? And what's going on?" Sam was desperately trying to get out of the green goop, but it was everywhere.

Luckily Merrin had just done a science project with an oral presentation on white blood cells. She had a feeling the green stuff was part of the immune system somehow.

As she observed her surroundings, Pearl wondered what she had gotten herself—and now Sam—into.

"Gross," Merrin muttered.

"Did you say 'gross,' Merrin? Do you know where we are?" Pearl asked.

"I think we are in Max's nose."

Then the walls surrounding them began to shudder.

"It feels like an EARTHQUAKE," Pearl tried to scream, but Merrin's yell was louder:

"HE'S GOING TO SNEEZE! HOLD ON!"

There was nothing to grab onto, so they hugged each other real tight. They jiggled and shook in all the green goop. The force was so tremendous that Pearl lost her grip on Merrin and was barely hanging onto Sam. She was quickly moving towards the light when the shaking finally stopped.

"Oh, Max, it will be okay. Let me wipe your nose," they heard their Aunt Lindsay say.

"*HURRY, SAM!* Pull Pearl in before the Kleenex gets her," Merrin shouted.

With all his strength, Sam pulled Pearl closer to them. Once Pearl was settled safely, Sam demanded, " Tell me what's going on! This is weird. And kinda smelly."

Merrin took a deep breath and said, "Well, we're in Max's nose and the green stuff is mucus."

"Mucus? You mean snot?" Sam interrupted.
"And don't tell me the green stuff has bugs in it."

"Uh, yeah. The bug invaders are some kind of bacteria or virus. The body has produced the mucus to trap the invaders so they can be sneezed out. You see the hair-like things? They're called cilia and they help move the mucus out. See how they're trying to wave?"

"This is going to be dirty detective work," Pearl said.

"Detective work?" Sam questioned.

"We're in Max's body because we need to find out what's wrong with him and make him feel better," Merrin answered. "We'd better keep moving. We don't want to waste any time. Sam, what was wrong with you when you were sick?"

"I had a bad cold and an ear infection," he answered as they were all being pushed further up the nose. They were headed towards the crime scene, where all the invaders were heading.

"Boy it's getting hot in here," Pearl commented. "Max must have a fever. Hey, look. What are those things?" Pearl pointed to some BUG LIKE creatures. They were small but they looked fierce and determined. It looked like some of them were starting to die, but some were escaping.

"*THOSE ARE THE BUG INVADERS!* The fever is killing some of them. The body will get super hot to destroy them, but it looks like some are getting away. Quick! Let's follow them," Merrin said.

Sam, who was starting to get into the whole scene, was getting a fast lead on the girls. As the girls told him to slow down they noticed some other animal-like creatures emerging from everywhere. It looked like they were chasing Sam!

"*SAM! LOOK OUT BEHIND YOU!*" the girls yelled.

It seemed like there were hundreds of them. When Sam finally realized something was chasing him, he ran faster and faster. He used some of his quick soccer moves to maneuver around them. It was terrifying to watch. Finally, Merrin realized what was going on.

"Those creatures are part of the immune system army. They're white blood cells, or leukocytes. Macrophages are a kind of white blood cell and are the first soldiers on the scene of a sickness. They're the powerhouses because they hunt down the invaders, suck them in and destroy them. They don't realize that Sam is not an invader. We need to do something, and fast!"

Panic and fear overwhelmed both girls, but they needed to think quickly before Sam got eaten up.

Hmmm... Merrin thought.

"Wait," Pearl said. "Let's get their attention and then try to tell them we're here to help." Pearl did not wait for a response and was on her way to make an ally.

"*SAM! SAM! SLOW DOWN!* Those macrophages are chasing you because they don't know who you are. They're going to eat you up! Wave to them and try to be their friend," Pearl yelled.

"Yikes!" Sam muttered.

Sam frantically waved to the yellow thing with the four arm-like limbs and a hungry-looking mouth.

It wasn't working. Pearl began to tremble, but that got her thinking. *What if...* **THAT WAS IT!** She just took her bold self right up to the macrophages and reached out her hand. One macrophage stopped and turned towards Pearl. Pearl right away began to explain that they were here to help make their baby cousin Max feel better for their holiday. Merrin and Sam watched in amazement as the macrophage immediately nodded with a smile and started to take off after some bacteria.

They knew there was no way they could keep up with the macrophages so Sam came up with a brilliant idea. He took off his belt and lassoed it around one of the passing macrophage's arms. Easier said than done. The belt slowly slipped from the arm he was aiming for. Sam watched in dismay, but just as suddenly as the belt slipped off one arm, it fell securely onto another.

"Phew," Sam said with relief.

The macrophage did not seem to mind being lassoed. He motioned them toward his back with one of his arms. They realized he was inviting them to hop on his back!

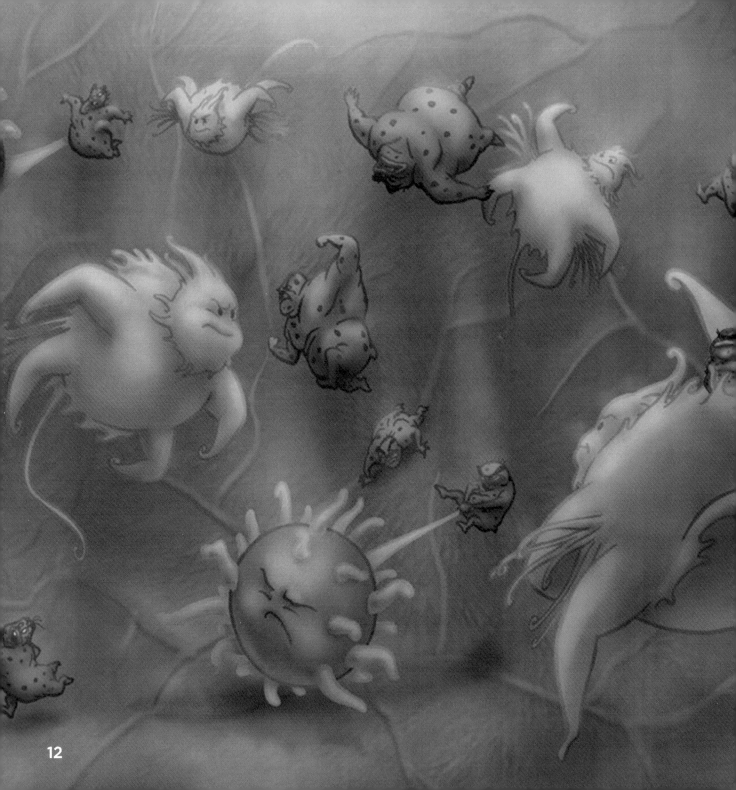

Sam whooped in delight as they all jumped on. Off they went, hanging tight to the macrophage, and each other, as the creature took off at lightning speed.

Pearl giggled with delight. "Let's call him *QUICKSTER*."

Suddenly, Merrin yelled, "*DUCK!*"

"*AHHHH!*" they all screamed.

QUICKSTER had sailed right underneath a dangling thing, obviously forgetting his passengers.

"Whoa. That was a close call," Sam said.

"Hey, that was the uvula. We must be in the mouth." Pearl remembered their last human body detective adventure through the digestive system.

They began to see a lot of commotion ahead and were cruising towards it. It grew dark again, but there was a soft light in the distance, similar to when they were in the nose. All of a sudden, out of nowhere, hundreds—maybe even thousands—of angry, mean-looking, bug-like creatures appeared.

"More invaders," Merrin said in a worried voice.

Sam looked excited about the imminent battle. This is fun, he thought to himself. *What a holiday!*

"Oh, look at Max pull his ear. It must be so sore." Aunt Lindsay's voice sounded muffled above the commotion.

Sam exclaimed, "*THAT'S IT!* We're in the ear. See the light? That must be the opening to the outside. *COOL!* But boy, my ear was killing me when I was sick. It would be great to help Max out."

It didn't look like there were enough macrophages to eat up all the bug invaders. What could be done?

Wait, thought Merrin. "*BACTERIA AND VIRUSES LOVE SUGAR!* Mom tells us not to eat too many candies since the sugar in the candies feeds the bugs and makes them stronger. Let's see if she's right by distracting them with some. Does anyone have any?"

Sam and Pearl looked at each other. Pearl looked really guilty. She was the queen of sneaking treats, but she was usually good about only having one. Or two.

"Well, I did have some, but I ate them on the plane." Pearl confessed.

"*LOOKY HERE.*" Sam said.

"Here's a lollypop I had for the plane ride." He threw it to Merrin.

Merrin immediately grabbed the candy and broke it into pieces. She then threw the pieces to the swarm of invaders. All at once, like mad and determined animals, they went crazy for it.

The bait was taken. The macrophages, realizing what was happening, took full advantage of the situation and swam off for the indulging invaders. They watched the attack as macrophages sucked the invaders in and swallowed them in loud gulps. It was a gruesome battle to watch, but a successful one. Well, almost successful...

Not all the invaders were killed. To make matters worse, some other ball-like creatures with many arms were approaching. What were they?

"*WAIT!*" Merrin yelled, "They're lymphocytes, another type of leukocyte or white blood cell. *YAY!* They must have sensed the battle and wanted to come help! Lymphocytes come from the bone marrow where they're made. They're the big guns, tough and fierce. *WOW!* They move fast. They'll help the macrophages destroy the rest of the invaders."

They watched in amazement as what Merrin said came true. Once it was all over, the unbearable heat subsided. It was quite astonishing.

Sam said, "Ahhh, it's so much cooler now. Seems like maybe the fever was a good thing and helped out."

"Mom always says fevers are really important because they kill bacteria and viruses. Now I see what she means," said Merrin.

Now the question was: *How would they get out of baby Max's ear?*

Without much discussion, Sam, acting like the general of their small group, commanded, "Okay, cousins, let's travel down the ear tube—not the scientific name, I suppose—but anyway, move toward the light, then *JUMP*."

The girls looked at each other and giggled at their cousin's authoritative manner and creative escape plan.

"'Eustachian tube' is the scientific name," Merrin informed Sam. "How about we just hold hands, think of all the great things we did to help Max, then wish ourselves back to our room?"

Without giving Sam a moment to veto that idea, Merrin and Pearl grabbed his hands. They felt relieved and content at a job well done as the dizziness settled in. It was a short trip and before they knew it they were back in their bedroom at the rental house in Mexico.

The rest of the cousins—Ben, Abby and Owen—came bursting through the door, startling them. They had exciting news.

"*MAX IS ALL BETTER!* It's like a miracle. He just stopped crying and is all happy now. Let's all go for a swim in the pool!" Abby exclaimed, while licking a lollypop.

"Sounds great." Sam smiled and winked at Merrin and Pearl. "But Abby, you might not want to eat that candy. The sugar in it feeds bacteria that can make you sick. Since that cold is going around, how about some sweet fun instead?"

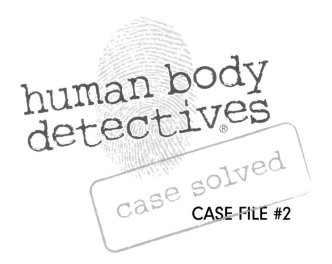

human body
detectives.®

case solved

CASE FILE #2

How good of a detective are you?

Can you find these two sneaky guys throughout the book?

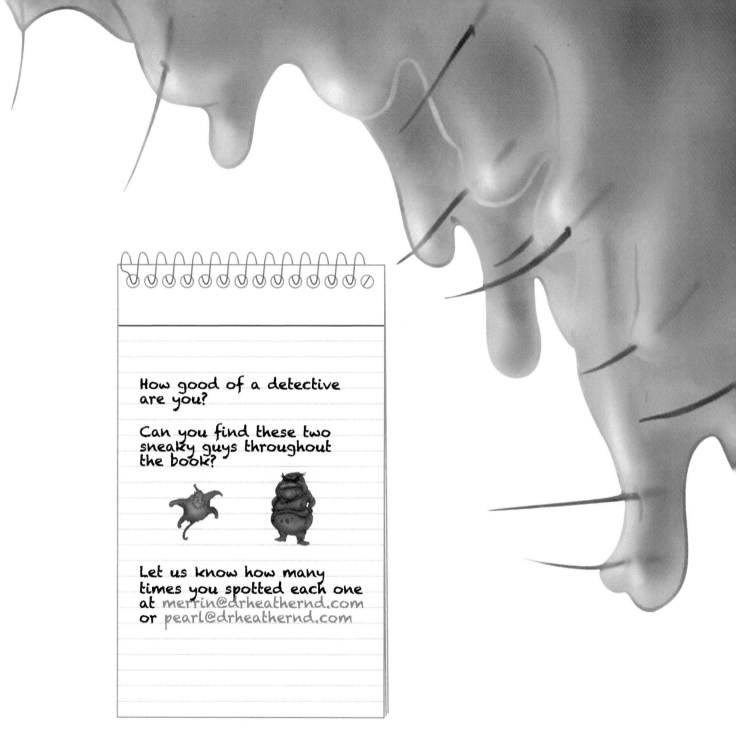

Let us know how many times you spotted each one at merrin@drheathernd.com or pearl@drheathernd.com

More About the Immune System

Human beings live with and are surrounded by billions of bacteria and viruses. Some are good and help our bodies, but some make us sick. Lucky for us — and not so lucky for the bad bugs — getting into the human body is not easy. These bug invaders will try to get through in many ways: through the skin, nose, mouth, ears or eyes. However, the body's immune system has incredible defense mechanisms designed to keep the invaders out: the skin is thick and hard to penetrate; the nose has cilia (fine little hairs) and goopy mucus that trap dirt and bugs; the eyes have tears that wash them away; and the mouth produces saliva and other chemicals the bugs do not like. These are the immune system's first line of defense.

I fought the bugs

and I won

Occasionally, bug invaders do break through this line of defense and enter the body, and when that happens the body works in even more amazing ways to protect itself. The brain sends an alert signal out to the immune system. This signal triggers inflammation, which causes the blood vessels to dilate and increase blood flow. When this happens, a team of white blood cells, or leukocytes (macrophages and lymphocytes), flocks to the scene of the crime. There are many types of white blood cells, including macrophages, lymphocytes, basophils, neutrophils, and eosinophils. The different white blood cells all have different jobs and come from different areas in the body such as the thymus, spleen, or bone marrow. They can travel through the blood but usually travel through a special system, efficiently designed just for them, called the lymphatic system.

Once at the invasion site, the white blood cells get to work doing their special jobs. For example, the macrophages will eat up the invaders, and the lymphocytes will not only help destroy the invaders, but will remember and recognize them, in case a similar bug comes in for a future attack. White blood cells are like little warriors floating around in your blood waiting to protect you from any **virus** or bacteria.

To help the immune system stay strong and healthy, it is very important to eat healthy, balanced meals full of **colorful** fruits and vegetables, and not too much sugar. The invaders love sugar as it makes them grow stronger and even multiply. It is also essential to get plenty of sleep,

have fun,

laugh a lot,

and be happy!

The Immune System

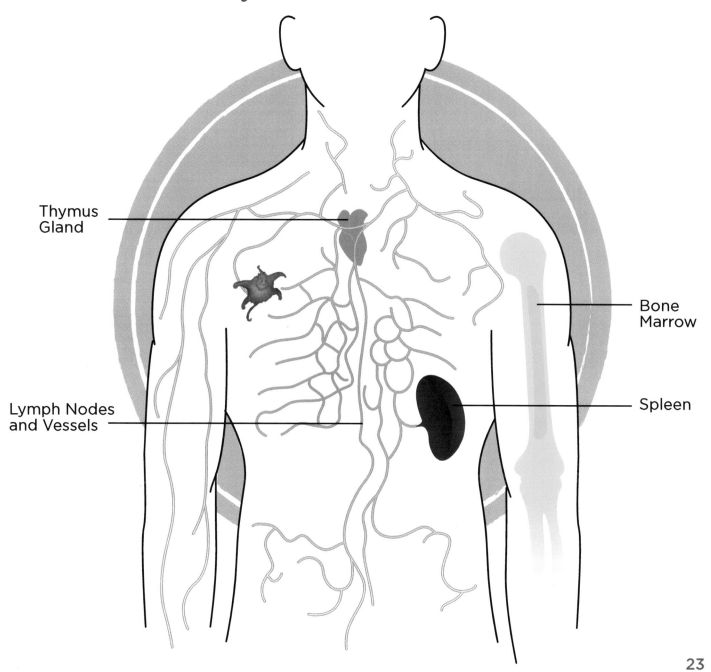

Thymus Gland

Bone Marrow

Lymph Nodes and Vessels

Spleen

Human B🦠dy Detectives Ask You...

These facts were news to Merrin, Pearl and Sam, so they wanted to share them with you.

did you know that...

- laughing lowers levels of stress hormones and strengthens the immune system?

- 6-year-olds laugh an average of 300 times a day and adults only laugh 15 to 100 times a day?

- it is impossible to sneeze with your eyes open?

- a cough releases an explosive charge of air that moves at speeds up to 60 mph?

- the air released in a sneeze can exceed 100 mph?

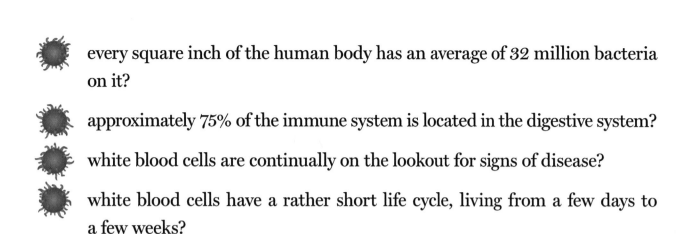

every square inch of the human body has an average of 32 million bacteria on it?

approximately 75% of the immune system is located in the digestive system?

white blood cells are continually on the lookout for signs of disease?

white blood cells have a rather short life cycle, living from a few days to a few weeks?

a drop of blood can contain anywhere from 7,000 to 25,000 white blood cells at a time?

if an invading infection fights back and persists, that number will significantly increase?

Your white blood cell count rises with infection as your body creates more "soldiers" to kill the disease.

an immunologist is a doctor who specializes in the immune system?

poor nutrition can weaken the immune system?

people who exercise have healthier immune systems?

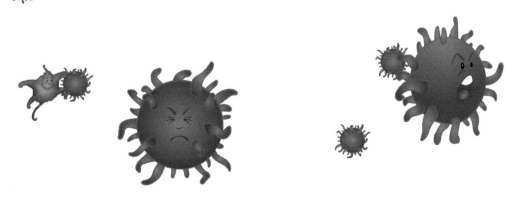

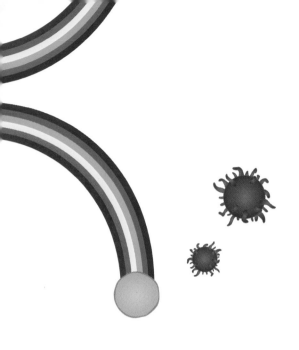

Be in Tune, Stay Immune

Boost up your immune system by eating a wide variety of **colorful**, whole foods (fruits and vegetables). The vivid colors in these foods mean they are full of nutrients, which help keep your white blood cells strong and powerful to fight off any unwanted invaders like bacteria or viruses.

Do you remember what you learned in the *The Lucky Escape* about all the differently colored foods and what they do in the body? Think about your next meal and how you might color up your plate. You could try adding blueberries and strawberries to your oatmeal, or lettuce and tomatoes to your sandwich.

Colorize Your Meals!

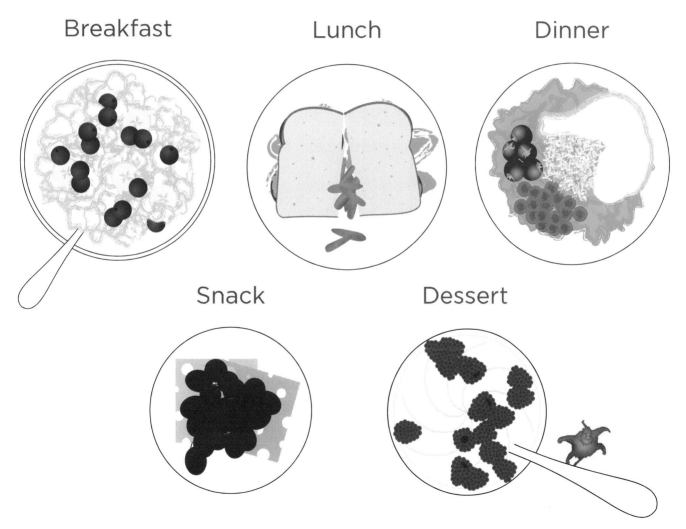

Breakfast

Lunch

Dinner

Snack

Dessert

27

Are you an Immune Buffoon?

Do chickens think rubber humans are funny?

What did the mother turkey tell the baby turkey when he ate too fast?
Stop gobblin' your food!

Why did the student eat his homework?
The teacher told him it was a piece of cake!

What did the left eye say to the right eye?
Between us, something smells!

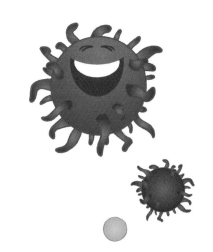

What has many ears but can't hear a thing?
A cornfield!

Why is your nose in the middle of your face?
Because it is in the scenter!

Why did the boy blush when he opened the fridge?
He saw the salad dressing!

What do you call a germ who wants to have a good time?
A FunGi! (a fun guy)

What did one tonsil say to the other?
"Get dressed. The doctor's taking us out tonight!"

What do you get if you cross a comedian with germs?
Sick jokes!

Did you hear the story about the germ?
Never mind. I don't want it spread all over!

Why did the germ cross the microscope?
To get to the other slide!

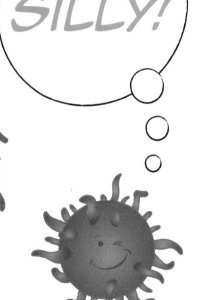

Knock Knock
Who's there?
Donut
Donut who?
Donut talk with your mouth full!

Glossary

A list of useful immune words and their meaning.

Bacteria (bac-TEER-ee-uh) Tiny organisms that can cause illnesses in the body.

Basophil (BAY-soh-fil) A type of white blood cell that is present when the body is inflamed (like when you sprain an ankle).

Bone Marrow (BOHN MAHR-oh) The tissue found inside your bones that is responsible for making blood cells, including white blood cells.

Cilia (SIL-ee-uh) Short, thin hairs located inside the nose and ears. They capture and try to push out things the body does not want.

Eosinophil (ee-oh-SIN-oh-fil) A type of white blood cell that fights infections from allergies and parasites.

Eustachian Tube (yoo-STAY-shan TOOB) The fancy, scientific word for the inside of your ear.

Fever (FEE-ver) An important immune response, a rise in body temperature that helps kill off unwanted bugs or bacteria.

Immune System (ih-MYOON SIS-tem) The system in the body responsible for identifying and fighting off unwanted bacteria, viruses, or other bugs. White blood cells play an important role in the immune system.

Leukocyte (LUKE-oh-site) Another name for white blood cell and a very important part of the immune system; a cell that helps protect the body against sickness. There are several different types of leukocytes, such as basophils, eosinophils, lymphocytes, macrophages, and neutrophils, all of which have different, specific jobs.

Lymphocyte (LIMF-oh-site) A type of white blood cell that is very important in helping your body be healthy. The lymphocyte has many jobs but one of them is to help the neutrophils fight viruses.

Lymphatic System (limf-AT-ik SIS-tem) The lymphatic system has two important jobs. First, it makes sure the fluids in the body are balanced, and second, it aids the immune system in defending against invading bacteria and viruses.

Macrophage (MAK-roh-fahj) A type of white blood cell that moves quickly to grab, suck in and kill any unwanted invasive material in the body.

Mucus (MYOO-kuss) A sticky, gooey substance found in the nose and other parts of the body, that traps bacteria and pushes it out of the body.

Neutrophil (NEW-troh-fil) A type of white blood cell that fights off viral infections, often one of the first at the scene of an infection.

Spleen (SPLEEN) The spleen is an organ located on the left side of your abdominal area, by your stomach. It is about the size of your fist and has many jobs, one of which is to help out the immune system by producing some of the white blood cells.

Thymus (THYE-muss) The thymus is an organ found just below your neck that produces some of your white blood cells.

Virus (VYE-russ) In Latin (an ancient language), "virus" means "poison." Like bacteria, viruses can cause illness in the body.

cucumbers are cool

Dr. Heather is a practicing naturopathic physician who promotes wellness and naturopathic healthcare on her website **drheathernd.com**. She is also the author of the award winning book series, *Human Body Detectives*. Dr. Heather lives on the Big Island of Hawaii with her husband and two daughters, and is currently at work on the next Human Body Detectives adventure.

 tweet with Dr. Heather on Twitter: twitter.com/drheathernd

Audio versions and apps of all the **Human Body Detectives** books—*Battle with the Bugs, The Lucky Escape* and *A Heart Pumping Adventure*, are available on iTunes.

Visit the **Human Body Detectives** website for free downloads, to view the HBD book trailers, and to watch Human Body Detectives Merrin and Pearl in the kitchen and visiting exciting places!

 visit us on Facebook: facebook.com/HumanBodyDetectives

LOOK FOR OTHER BOOKS IN THE HUMAN BODY DETECTIVE SERIES:
The Lucky Escape and *A Heart Pumping Adventure.*

kids are saying

"It was exciting. I felt like I was in the story myself."
Maxine, age 9

"My favorite part was when they were fighting the bugs. It was very exciting."
Cooper, age 7

adults are saying

"Someone gave me Dr. Heather's first book on the digestive system and my daughter learned so much from it. When her new book came out on the immune system, it was an easy purchase for me."
Mark, father

*"It is, to be honest, **one of the most interesting and engaging human body learning tools** I've come across in a very long time."*
ourbigearth.com

The series helps us be proactive about health by providing a fun, engaging way to teach the concepts to our children. Overall, we're impressed. The series is a great way to help your children become more aware of their bodies and how the foods they eat can affect them. Hopefully, in turn, they'll be able to make healthy food choices in the future."
kindervibe.ca

www.humanbodydetectives.com

CPSIA information can be obtained
at www.ICGtesting.com
Printed in the USA
266972LV00002B

456·3